To:

_____

From:

_____

Message:

_____

_____

_____

101
PRAYERS
for my SON

Rob & Joanna Teigen

CHRISTIAN ART
PUBLISHERS

Published by Christian Art Publishers
PO Box 1599, Vereeniging, 1930, RSA

© 2016
First edition 2016

Cover designed by Christian Art Publishers

Images used under license from Shutterstock.com

Printed in China

ISBN 978-1-4321-1347-6

16 17 18 19 20 21 22 23 24 25 – 10 9 8 7 6 5 4 3 2 1

Children are a heritage
from the LORD, offspring a
reward from Him.
Psalm 127:3

01

Quiet Rest

The LORD is my shepherd, I lack nothing. He makes me lie down in green pastures, He leads me beside quiet waters, He refreshes my soul.

Psalm 23:1-3

Lord God,

My son is overwhelmed by a hectic schedule and the pressure to succeed. Call him away from the busyness and give him quiet rest. Refresh his soul and renew his strength. Help him to remember once again how You provide everything he needs. Set him free from working and striving on his own – let him be still and know that You are God. Soothe his spirit as he quiets himself in Your presence. Amen.

02

Self-Control

Better a patient person than a warrior, one
with self-control than one who takes a city.
Proverbs 16:32

Lord God,

My son needs Your help to cope with
frustration and disappointment. Guard his
heart from anger when he can't have his
way. Keep him from lashing out with harsh
words or his fists when he's upset. Give him
self-control beyond his years, so he can
act in love instead of reacting in hate.
Fill him with patience, soothing away any
aggression that would create destruction
in his life. Amen.

03

Overcoming Bullying

I put no trust in my bow, my sword does not
bring me victory; but You give us victory over
our enemies, You put our adversaries to shame.
Psalm 44:6-7

Father,

You know better than anyone if my son is
being bullied. Give him strength when
bullies threaten his safety, his confidence
and his peace. Defend my son from his
enemies. Crush any plans to harm his body,
his reputation or his self-respect. Surround
him with protection and support. Build his
courage to face any threat, trusting that
You are by his side. Thank You for Your
faithful love and power to save. Amen.

04

Wise Choices

A foolish son brings grief to his father and
bitterness to the mother who bore him.
Proverbs 17:25

Holy Lord,

My son's choices may bring honor and
joy to our family, or cause heartache and
pain. Give him discernment in choosing
his friends. Keep him from impulsive
decisions leading to trouble or shame.
Teach him integrity, respect and self-control
so he is worthy of trust. Set him free from
regret and a lost reputation by keeping
him on the path of wisdom. Guide his
steps each day. Amen.

05

Loving His Future Wife

*Husbands, love your wives and
do not be harsh with them.*
Colossians 3:19

Lord,

Prepare my son to one day be a loving
husband. Give him a patient heart, full of
compassion for his bride. Make him
reasonable – free from selfish demands and
expectations. Let him become the kind of
man to forgive her faults, show sensitivity
for her feelings, and cherish her each day.
Help him to show her Your love through my
son's tender care. Amen.

06

Prayer Life

Rejoice always, pray continually, give
thanks in all circumstances; for this is
God's will for you in Christ Jesus.
1 Thessalonians 5:16-18

Father,

Teach my son how to pray. Let him
celebrate life's joys by thanking You and
praising Your name. When troubles come,
let him bring his needs to You. If he's
confused about which way to go, let him
seek You for wisdom and direction. Move
him to pray for healing, understanding,
and strength. Display Your power and
faithfulness as You respond to the prayers
of my child. Amen.

07

Peace of God

Do not be anxious about anything, but in every situation, by prayer and petition, with thanksgiving, present your requests to God. And the peace of God, which transcends all understanding, will guard your hearts and your minds in Christ Jesus.

Philippians 4:6-7

Lord,

Worry and stress are stealing peace from my son. Teach him to bring his problems to You in prayer. Show Your loving power to provide for his needs and fix what's broken in his life. Give him faith to believe that You hear and respond when he reaches out to You. Relieve his anxious thoughts and soothe his spirit as he trusts in You. Guard his heart and mind with Your peace. Amen.

08

Dreams and Vision

Take delight in the LORD, and He will
give you the desires of your heart.
Psalm 37:4

Father God,

My son is excited about where his future
may lead. Careers, romance, adventure –
he can't wait to use his talents and explore
the world. Fill him with eagerness to discover
Your perfect will for his life. Let him pursue
You with all his heart, finding his greatest joy
in knowing Jesus. As he commits his way to
You, satisfy his hopes and dreams out of Your
great love. Thank You for all You have in
store for him. Amen.

09

Pure Words

Among you there must not be even a hint of
sexual immorality, or of any kind of impurity,
or of greed, because these are improper for
God's holy people. Nor should there be
obscenity, foolish talk or coarse joking, which
are out of place, but rather thanksgiving.

Ephesians 5:3-4

Father,

Teach my son how to please You with his
words. Guard his mouth from profanity or
crude humor. Let him speak words of
kindness and respect for girls and women.
Give him maturity to avoid gossip, slander,
arguing or complaining. Fill his conversations
with thankfulness, honesty and goodness.
Let his words be a testimony of faith and
his place in Your family. Amen.

10

The Ability to Listen

Listen, my son, to your father's instruction
and do not forsake your mother's teaching.
They are a garland to grace your head and a
chain to adorn your neck.

Proverbs 1:8-9

Heavenly Father,

Protect my role of influence in my son's
life. Give me words of wisdom to teach
him Your ways. Keep him willing and open
to receive advice, correction and help.
Pour out rewards in his life as he listens to
my counsel. Build trust between us so I can
continue to walk by his side as he grows.
Make me worthy of the leadership You've
entrusted to me, and use me as a
blessing in his life. Amen.

11

A Heart of Grace

Make sure that nobody pays back wrong
for wrong, but always strive to do what is
good for each other and for everyone else.
1 Thessalonians 5:15

Lord God,

Thank You for Your mercy and forgiveness
when we fail. Give my son Your heart of
grace for others. Keep him from retaliating
and seeking revenge when he's wronged.
Make him a peacemaker when he's
tempted to fight for his rights. Fill him with
love by Your Spirit so he's concerned with
others as much as himself. Let goodness rule
his heart and mind in every situation. Amen.

12

Seeking Forgiveness

Therefore, there is now no condemnation
for those who are in Christ Jesus.
Romans 8:1

Lord,

My son is struggling to confess and forgive
himself for having sinned against You.
Renew his hope in Your loving forgiveness.
Help him to believe Your promise to cast
his sin as far as the east is from the west,
remembering it no more. Let him rest by
knowing that Your grace is enough – no
matter what anyone says, he is clean and
whole in Your eyes. Amen.

13

Hard Work

Whatever you do, work at it with all your heart, as working for the Lord, not for human masters, since you know that you will receive an inheritance from the Lord as a reward. It is the Lord Christ you are serving.

Colossians 3:23-24

Father,

You know the tasks my son needs to accomplish – homework, chores, practices, commitments – and his struggle to face the challenges. Give him strength to tackle his work with a willing heart. Motivate him to do his best and to finish what he starts. As he learns discipline, let him experience the reward for a job well done. May he seek to please You in all he does, seeking Your glory above his own. Amen.

14

The Path of Purity

How can a young person stay on the path of purity? By living according to Your word. I seek You with all my heart; do not let me stray from Your commands.

Psalm 119:9-10

Lord,

Fill my son with a passion for You and Your Word. Teach him Your ways so he can remain pure in a world bent on stealing his innocence. Let the Scriptures be his truth and his guide as he grows. Give him wisdom and strength to resist temptation. Be his one desire, and may he keep his eyes fixed on You so he can obey You in everything. Amen.

15

Good Friends

The righteous choose their friends carefully,
but the way of the wicked leads them astray.
Proverbs 12:26

Lord God,

My son's friends hold tremendous
influence in his life. Give him wisdom to
seek out those who will encourage him
in following You. Surround him with
examples of integrity, self-control and
kindness. Protect him from those who reject
Your Word and tempt him to sin. Keep him
from compromising his values to fit in or to
avoid feeling lonely. Let him hold on to You,
his most faithful Friend of all. Amen.

16

Safety and Protection

For in the day of trouble He will keep me safe
in His dwelling; He will hide me in the shelter of
His sacred tent and set me high upon a rock.

Psalm 27:5

Lord and Savior,

This world holds many dangers for my son.
Keep him safe from accidents, illness and
injury. Protect him from anyone who would
abuse or exploit his innocence. Guard him
from false teachers who would deny Your
truth and discourage his faith. Shield him
from gossip and slander, loneliness and
rejection. Be his mighty Guardian and
peaceful shelter wherever he goes.
Amen.

17

Living in Humility

Live in harmony with one another. Do not be
proud, but be willing to associate with people
of low position. Do not be conceited.

Romans 12:16

Holy Lord,

Thank You for loving us just as we are.
Give my son Your heart of compassion
towards everyone. Let him be caring,
reaching out to the lonely and marginalized.
Guard his heart from pride that pursues its
own popularity and image. Make him a
peacemaker, building unity by his example
of kindness and respect. Give him eyes that
see past the surface, and value each
person as Your special creation. Amen.

18

Gentleness and Compassion

Therefore, as God's chosen people, holy and
dearly loved, clothe yourselves with compassion,
kindness, humility, gentleness and patience.
Colossians 3:12

Lord,

In a world that celebrates toughness and
aggression, fill my son with gentleness by
Your Spirit. Give him compassion for animals
and little children. Help him to respect the
elderly and to show empathy for those who
suffer handicaps. Make him patient with his
siblings and troubled students at school.
Use his strength to defend the weak and
vulnerable, and teach him the power
of love. Amen.

19

Boldness and Confidence

Then they called them in again and commanded them not to speak or teach at all in the name of Jesus. But Peter and John replied, "Which is right in God's eyes: to listen to you, or to Him? You be the judges! As for us, we cannot help speaking about what we have seen and heard."

Acts 4:18-20

Heavenly Father,

You tell us to count the cost of following Jesus. No matter how the world resists You, give my son a bold witness for the gospel. Guard him from fear or discouragement when he's called a fool or suffers for his faith. Let him speak Your Word and uphold Your truth, no matter the opposition. May his love for Christ always triumph over intimidation by Your enemies. Amen.

20

True Generosity

Each of you should give what you have decided
in your heart to give, not reluctantly or under
compulsion, for God loves a cheerful giver.
2 Corinthians 9:7

Lord God,

My son's heart is revealed by his money and
possessions. Fill him with gladness in giving
to You. Let him demonstrate God's love by
relieving poverty and meeting the needs
of others. When he's tempted to hoard his
blessings for himself, replace his greed with
generosity. Teach him the powerful lesson
that when we give, we receive even
more from You. Amen.

21

Honesty and Truth

Whoever would love life and see good days
must keep their tongue from evil and their
lips from deceitful speech.

1 Peter 3:10

My Lord and God,

Make my son a man of his word. Set
him free from the traps of keeping secrets,
covering his tracks or exaggerating his
accomplishments. Give him courage to
face hard consequences instead of
denying his mistakes. Make him a truth-
teller, building trust in every relationship.
Keep him honest so his testimony of Your
truth is never compromised. Amen.

22

Contentment and Joy

The love of money is a root of all kinds
of evil. Some people, eager for money,
have wandered from the faith and
pierced themselves with many griefs.
1 Timothy 6:10

Father,

In the troubles and stresses of life, guard my
son from depending on money for comfort
or security. Deliver him from the temptation
of chasing after financial success. Spare him
the pain and disappointment of looking for
satisfaction in material things. He can't serve
both money and Jesus – unite his heart to
Yours so he loves You above everything else.
Let him be joyful and content with all You've
provided for him. Amen.

23

A Virtuous Life

"I made a covenant with my eyes not to
look lustfully at a young woman."
Job 31:1

Lord God,

Teach my son to cherish the girls You've
created. Let him respect young women
with his words, thoughts and attitudes.
Train his eyes to look at what's pure and
to turn away from temptation. Give him
Your love that protects, honors and builds
up the young women in his life. Let him
commit his way to You. Amen.

24

Being Kind and Helpful

Do everything without grumbling or arguing,
so that you may become blameless and pure,
"children of God without fault in a warped
and crooked generation."
Philippians 2:14-15

Father,

Teach my son how valuable he is to our
family and his community. Give him a
willing heart to do his part without
complaining. Let him show respect by
obeying instructions without argument.
Make it a joy for him to listen and learn, to
pitch in and do his work. Bless him with a
reputation for a kind and helpful attitude.
Use him to show Your love to others as he
submits to Your will each day. Amen.

25

A Team Player

Do nothing out of selfish ambition or vain conceit. Rather, in humility value others above yourselves, not looking to your own interests but each of you to the interests of the others.

Philippians 2:3 4

Lord Jesus,

In our "me-first" culture, my son may be tempted to think only of himself. Put to rest his efforts to be the most popular or the one in charge. Make him humble so he doesn't crave attention, praise and blessings for himself alone. Teach him to be a team player – encouraging the talents and success of everyone in his life. Guard his heart from selfishness that tears others down. Let him love as You love him. Amen.

26

Witnessing to Others

Sing to the LORD, all the earth; proclaim
His salvation day after day. Declare His
glory among the nations, His marvelous
deeds among all peoples.

1 Chronicles 16:23-24

Heavenly Father,

Tell Your story of salvation through my son's
life. Use him to declare the power of Your
deliverance from the enemy. Give him a
voice to speak the truth of Your Word to all
who would listen. Fill his mouth with praise
for all the ways You protect and provide. Let
him celebrate victory over sin and darkness.
Use my son as a mighty messenger of Your
gospel to this lost and hurting world. Amen.

27

Endurance and Fortitude

Even youths grow tired and weary, and
young men stumble and fall; but those who
hope in the LORD will renew their strength.

Isaiah 40:30-31

Lord,

My son is weary of working hard and
submitting to what's required of him.
The rewards seem out of reach. He's not
sure that it's worth it to keep doing the
right thing. Give him Your strength, and
encourage his heart to keep going.
Help him to resist temptation to sin or
doubt Your goodness. Surround him with
support and build him up with Your Word.
Keep him steady and faithful as he puts
his hope in You. Amen.

28

A Discerning Heart

Teach me knowledge and good judgment,
for I trust Your commands.
Psalm 119:66

Lord God,

My son has so many choices ahead of
him – classes, careers, relationships, financial
decisions – without Your help he won't know
which way to go. Deepen his knowledge of
Your Word so he knows what's right. Fill him
with Your Spirit so he conforms his plans to
Your will. Give him good sense and insight
beyond his years as he navigates the road
ahead. Let him love You and seek to please
You in everything he does. Amen.

29

Justice and Integrity

Speak up for those who cannot speak for
themselves, for the rights of all who are
destitute. Speak up and judge fairly;
defend the rights of the poor and needy.
Proverbs 31:8-9

Righteous Lord,

Raise up my son to be a champion for the
weak. Give him courage to speak up for
the persecuted and oppressed. Let him
stand up against bullies and liars, abusers
and law-breakers. Use my son to bring
justice to his school, community and this
world. Bless him with resources to relieve
suffering and poverty. Build him up in the
knowledge of Your truth so he can stand
firm for what's right. Amen.

30

The Future Love of His Life

A wife of noble character who can find?
She is worth far more than rubies.
Her husband has full confidence in her and
lacks nothing of value. She brings him good,
not harm, all the days of her life.

Proverbs 31:10-12

Father,

I pray for the gift of a godly wife for my son
one day. May she have a deep devotion to
Jesus so Your love will flow through her life to
her family. Prepare her to help and support
my son one day. Help her to be faithful and
wise, respectful and kind. Even now, protect
her and keep her close to You. Amen.

31

A Strong Faith

Jesus said to her, "I am the resurrection and the life. The one who believes in Me will live, even though they die; and whoever lives by believing in Me will never die. Do you believe this?"

John 11:25-26

Lord,

Give my son an unshakable faith in Jesus. Persuade him by Your Spirit that Your Word is the truth. Fill him with joy as he looks ahead to eternity with You. When his beliefs are challenged, give him confidence in Christ. Rescue him from doubt and discouragement in times of trouble. Let him find his life – his hope, his purpose and his salvation – by trusting in Jesus with all his heart. Amen.

32

His Self-Esteem

You created my inmost being; You knit me together in my mother's womb. I praise You because I am fearfully and wonderfully made; Your works are wonderful, I know that full well.

Psalm 139:13-14

Lord Jesus,

My son has a tendency to compare himself to others, leaving him feeling insecure. He feels like he can never measure up to everyone else. Help him to remember that he is Your own special creation. You planned his personality, his mind, his talents and his smile before You even made the world. Give him significance by knowing that he is Yours. Soothe his wounded heart, and silence the lies that say he's not good enough. Amen.

33

Gladness and Fulfillment

What causes fights and quarrels among you?
Don't they come from your desires that battle
within you? You desire but do not have, so you
kill. You covet but you cannot get what you
want, so you quarrel and fight. You do not have
because you do not ask God.

James 4:1-2

Heavenly Father,

My son has become very competitive,
always fighting for first place. It's costing him
peace, friends and his own character as he
insists on winning all the time. Remind him
of his blessings. Teach him contentment. Let
him learn to pray when he has a need or
desire. Set him free from competition and
jealousy, and fill him with patience and love.
Amen.

34

Freedom from Fears

When I am afraid, I put my trust in You.
In God, whose word I praise – in God
I trust and am not afraid.

Psalm 56:3-4

Holy Lord,

Fear is keeping my son from exploring new
friendships, experiences and opportunities.
Set him free from doubt and insecurity that
keep him from walking in Your will. Fill his
mind with truth – You are his strength, shield
and hope. Give him courage as he trusts
that You are always by his side. Build his
faith to believe in Your love that never fails.
Let him be controlled by Your Spirit instead
of his anxiety. Amen.

35

Patience and a Quiet Spirit

My dear brothers and sisters, take note of
this: Everyone should be quick to listen,
slow to speak and slow to become angry,
because human anger does not produce
the righteousness that God desires.

James 1:19-20

Father,

Sometimes my son's temper will explode
at the smallest provocation. His touchy
emotions, hasty arguments and refusal
to listen create trouble in his life. Quiet his
spirit so he will listen patiently. Give him
compassion and kindness to soften his
heart towards others. Set him free from the
trap of anger so his relationships can
flourish in peace. Fill him with the love of
Jesus for everyone. Amen.

36

A Hunger for God

"So I say to you: Ask and it will be given to you; seek and you will find; knock and the door will be opened to you. For everyone who asks receives; the one who seeks finds; and to the one who knocks, the door will be opened."

Luke 11:9-10

Father God,

My son needs You more than anything this world can offer. Create a longing in his heart for You that never ends. Bring him to his knees in prayer with every question and doubt in his mind. Let him cry out for strength and help when he's overwhelmed by trouble. Be his wisdom when he asks which way to go. May he discover Your love and faithfulness as he reaches out and finds You're always there. Amen.

37

Submission to Authority

Let everyone be subject to the governing
authorities, for there is no authority except
that which God has established. The authorities
that exist have been established by God.

Romans 13:1

Lord Jesus,

My son needs wisdom and self-control to
submit to the laws of our country and
community. Help him to trust that boundaries
are for his good, to protect him from harm.
Let him show respect to police officers and
public servants. Reward him with a reputation
for integrity and maturity. Use him as an
example of obedience among his peers.
Thank You for caring for him through our
leaders. Amen.

38

Wisdom and Discernment

If any of you lacks wisdom, you should ask God, who gives generously to all without finding fault, and it will be given to you.

James 1:5

O Lord,

You know my son's confusion about which path to take. Help him to seek You for wisdom and insight as he makes decisions. Give him confidence in Your promise to show him which way he should go. Fill him with patience by Your Spirit, trusting that You'll give him just what he needs at the proper time. Help him to love You and to pursue Your will and Your ways each step of his journey. Amen.

39

Defeating Temptation

In the same way, count yourselves dead to sin but alive to God in Christ Jesus. Therefore do not let sin reign in your mortal body so that you obey its evil desires. You have been set free from sin and have become slaves to righteousness.

Romans 6:11-12, 18

Heavenly Father,

It's tempting to depend on the pleasures of this world to ease our pain and relieve our stress. Give my son wisdom to see that alcohol, food, drugs, sex, money and relationships can never meet the needs of his heart. Protect him from the destruction that addiction could bring to his life. Let him love You, and depend on Your comfort and strength. May he live in freedom as he follows You. Amen.

40

Willing Obedience

Children, obey your parents in the Lord, for this
is right. "Honor your father and mother" – which
is the first commandment with a promise –
"so that it may go well with you and that you
may enjoy long life on the earth."

Ephesians 6:1-3

O Lord,

Thank You for the gift of parenthood and
the blessing of my son. Help him to value
my role as provider, protector and helper in
his life. Give him self-control so he can obey
and speak with respect. Reward him for
submitting to my discipline and guidance.
Teach me wisdom, love and faithfulness so
that I'm worthy of his honor. Give my son a
future that's rich in Your goodness. Amen.

41

Stress and Anxiety

When I said, "My foot is slipping," Your unfailing
love, LORD, supported me. When anxiety was great
within me, Your consolation brought me joy.

Psalm 94:18-19

Lord,

My son is often overcome by fear and
insecurity. As much as he tries to play it
safe and stay in control, peace is out of
reach. Help him to depend on You for his
life. Let him lean on Your strength when he
faces danger, disappointment or failure.
Build him up in Your love. Restore his joy as
he sees You're always near and forever
faithful. Amen.

42

Sobriety and Self-Restraint

Do not be foolish, but understand what the
Lord's will is. Do not get drunk on wine, which
leads to debauchery. Instead, be filled with the
Spirit, speaking to one another with psalms,
hymns, and songs from the Spirit.

Ephesians 5:17-19

Holy Lord,

My son will be tempted to use alcohol or
drugs to have fun, fit in with the crowd, or
cope with stress. Give him wisdom to
recognize the dangers of getting drunk or
high. Strengthen him to resist any pressure
to party or break the law. Let him depend
on You for comfort during difficult times.
Fill him with Your Spirit so he can live a life
of worship and obedience. Amen.

43

Perseverance and Diligence

A sluggard's appetite is never filled, but the
desires of the diligent are fully satisfied.
Proverbs 13:4

Lord Jesus,

My son is tired – he's lost the motivation to
set goals, work hard and try new things.
Spur him on to work hard and stay active.
Sharpen his mind, and make him curious
and eager to learn. Stir up his energy to
tackle his responsibilities and do his best.
Show him the wonderful rewards You
hold for his diligent efforts. Amen.

44

Good Advice

Plans fail for lack of counsel, but with
many advisers they succeed.
Proverbs 15:22

Lord,

My son needs guidance as he navigates
the road ahead. Surround him with mature
believers to speak words of love, truth and
wisdom into his life. Give him a humble
heart, one that is eager to ask for help and
advice. Allow his plans to prosper as he
earnestly seeks to do the right thing.
Let him walk in obedience and truth
each day of his life. Amen.

45

A Giving Heart

Command them to do good, to be rich in good
deeds, and to be generous and willing to share.
1 Timothy 6:18

Lord and Savior,

You've lavished Your love on my son
and given him too many blessings to
count. Teach him to share with others as
You share Your love and kindness with
him. Keep him from a selfish attitude
that thinks only of itself. Fill his heart with
joy when he helps others and gives
generously. Let him shine Your light in
the world – easing pain, loneliness and
poverty – out of love for You. Amen.

46

Knowing the Truth

See to it that no one takes you captive through
hollow and deceptive philosophy, which depends
on human tradition and the elemental spiritual
forces of this world rather than on Christ.

Colossians 2:8

Father,

Persuasive voices will challenge my son's
trust in Your Word. Give him an unshakable
faith in Jesus to withstand any attack on
his faith. Supply him with discernment to
recognize teachings or traditions that
contradict the Bible. Help him to resist the
temptation to conform to the culture instead
of the truth. In these days where believers
are insulted and persecuted, strengthen
him to stand firm. Amen.

47

Christian Friends

Do not be yoked together with unbelievers.
For what do righteousness and wickedness
have in common? Or what fellowship can
light have with darkness?

2 Corinthians 6.14

Lord,

Thank You for the gift of friendship.
Help my son to understand the powerful
influence friends hold in his allegiance to
You. Surround my son with strong believers
who are committed to Christ and obey Your
Word. Protect him from falling in with anyone
who will discourage his faith and obedience.
Use my son's own kindness and faithfulness
to build up the friends in his life. Amen.

48

Clean Living

Finally, brothers and sisters,
whatever is true, whatever is noble, whatever is
right, whatever is pure, whatever is lovely,
whatever is admirable – if anything is excellent
or praiseworthy – think about such things.

Philippians 4:8

Father God,

My son needs the mind of Jesus as he
chooses the games, books and entertainment that fill his time. Guide him by Your
Spirit to value wholesome humor, honorable
heroes and biblical truth in whatever he's
reading and watching. Teach him to
discipline his thoughts, dwelling on what's
good and admirable in the world You've
made. Let him please You in everything as
he keeps his mind fixed on You. Amen.

49

Wholesome Speech

Do not let any unwholesome talk come out
of your mouths, but only what is helpful for
building others up according to their needs,
that it may benefit those who listen.

Ephesians 4:29

Righteous Lord,

My son's words have the power to
encourage and help or to tear others
down. Use my son to share the love of
Jesus when he speaks. Guard him from
gossip, insults or critical remarks that
can only do harm. Give him sensitivity
to care when others are hurting so he
can share a word of comfort. Let him
inspire courage when someone is
afraid. Enable him to share Your Word
so the lost can be found in You. Amen.

50

Hope in God

Yet he did not waver through unbelief
regarding the promise of God, but was
strengthened in his faith and gave glory to
God, being fully persuaded that God had
power to do what He had promised.
Romans 4:20-21

Father,

When troubles come and the future is
uncertain, my son can doubt that You're
there. Give him faith that stands through
any storm. Let him believe in Your promises
to protect and provide. Fix his hope on
eternity with You, knowing that in the end
You'll make everything right. Help him to
know You're always in control, trusting in
the powerful, invisible God instead of
what his eyes can see. Amen.

51

Encouragement and Hope

He said to me, "My grace is sufficient for you,
for My power is made perfect in weakness."
Therefore I will boast all the more gladly
about my weaknesses, so that Christ's
power may rest on me

2 Corinthians 12:9

Lord Jesus,

My son feels discouraged. Things don't
always go as planned and failure weakens
his confidence. Thank You for offering Your
strength whenever he needs help. Teach him
to depend on You for wisdom and strength.
Be glorified in his life as he lives in Your grace
and help him to be encouraged by Your
promises for his life. Amen.

52

Discipline and Control

No discipline seems pleasant at the time,
but painful. Later on, however, it produces
a harvest of righteousness and peace for
those who have been trained by it.
Hebrews 12:11

Lord God,

My son is struggling to accept the
consequences for his actions. Help him
understand that discipline will build him up,
making him more like Jesus. Give him
wisdom to see how correction is an act of
love – it sets him free to grow and learn.
Bring peace to his heart as he takes
responsibility for his behavior. Give me
wisdom in training him to know right from
wrong, according to Your Word. Amen.

53

Honorable Pursuits

For everything in the world – the lust
of the flesh, the lust of the eyes, and the pride
of life – comes not from the Father but from the
world. The world and its desires pass away,
but whoever does the will of God lives forever.
1 John 2:16-17

Heavenly Father,

My son craves new things and experiences.
He longs to be popular. Give him a stronger,
deeper love for You than any other desire
in this world. Show him that none of his
passions will satisfy, except living in Your
perfect will. When he's tempted to chase
after popularity, draw him back to You.
Be his greatest joy in this life as he looks
forward to eternity with You. Amen.

54

Freedom from Jealousy

"You shall not covet your neighbor's wife.
You shall not set your desire on your
neighbor's house or land, his male or female
servant, his ox or donkey, or anything that
belongs to your neighbor."
Deuteronomy 5:21

Father,

My son is caught in the trap of comparison –
he's jealous of others' talents, material
possessions and opportunities. Change his
heart to hold love instead of resentment
when his friends are blessed. Fill him with
gratitude for all the good You've done in
his life. Keep him content with what he has
today, trusting You'll give him all he needs in
the future. Set him free from envy so he can
praise Your name. Amen.

55

Grudges and Unforgiveness

Bear with each other and forgive one another
if any of you has a grievance against someone.
Forgive as the Lord forgave you.

Colossians 3:13

Lord,

It's painful to be left out, let down, or
laughed at. Every time my son's trust is
broken, he puts up a wall to protect himself
from further pain. Soften his heart to forgive.
Let him see the good in others and show
patience for their weakness. Heal his wounds
and give him gratitude for Your mercy and
grace, granting him the ability to love as
You love him. Amen.

56

A Loving Heart

For this is the message you heard from the
beginning: We should love one another.
Anyone who hates a brother or sister is a
murderer, and you know that no murderer
has eternal life residing in him.

1 John 3:11, 15

Lord God,

We love because You first loved us.
Move in my son's hard heart and melt his
hateful feelings away. When he's tempted
to criticize, take revenge and lash out in
anger, bring Your peace. Give him love like
Yours that doesn't demand payment or
perfection. As he trusts You for forgiveness
and salvation, fill him with kindness and
patience by Your Spirit. Let him be known
as a man of grace. Amen.

57

Spiritual Purity

When someone tells you to consult mediums
and spiritists, who whisper and mutter, should
not a people inquire of their God? Why consult
the dead on behalf of the living?

Isaiah 8:19

Holy Father,

Protect my son from the enemy's
enticement to explore the power of
darkness. Give him wisdom to reject
any elements of magic or the occult.
Teach him the foolishness of consulting
horoscopes or fortune-tellers instead
of You. Let him trust in Your power and
authority – Your name is above any
name in heaven or on earth or under
the earth. Keep him close to You in
prayer and be his strength. Amen.

58

Spiritual Gifts

There are different kinds of gifts, but the same Spirit distributes them. There are different kinds of service, but the same Lord. There are different kinds of working, but in all of them and in everyone it is the same God at work.

1 Corinthians 12:4-6

Lord God,

Thank You for equipping us to serve You and love others in Your name. Give my son a desire to do God's work. Help him to discover his gifts from the Spirit so he can fulfill his role in Your church. Let him find joy, whether teaching, serving or helping, as You empower him to do all You ask. May his work and service be an expression of worship and love for You. Amen.

59

Faithfulness and Integrity

"Whoever can be trusted with very little
can also be trusted with much, and
whoever is dishonest with very little will
also be dishonest with much."

Luke 16:10

Father,

I pray that my son would grow in
responsibility as he grows in years. Give
him integrity as he handles his work and his
money. Let him keep his promises and follow
through with his commitments. Make him
dependable when he's trusted with personal
information or someone's private feelings.
Help him to be punctual, thorough and
respectful, earning respect wherever
he goes. Amen.

60

A Good Education

The heart of the discerning
acquires knowledge, for the ears
of the wise seek it out.
Proverbs 18:15

Lord,

Give my son a grateful heart for the gift
of education. Keep his mind alert and
curious, eager to learn new things.
Help him to be diligent in his studies when
he's tired, bored or challenged. Keep
him from pride so he'll ask questions and
seek help when he's struggling. Provide
capable, caring teachers to guide him
along the way. Build him up in wisdom
and knowledge day by day. Amen.

61

His Reputation

A good name is more desirable
than great riches; to be esteemed
is better than silver or gold.

Proverbs 22:1

Holy Lord,

A good name is difficult to achieve and
so very easy to lose. Keep my son from
foolish choices that lead to shame and
embarrassment. Guard his words from
gossip and lies that break trust with others.
Give him wisdom in choosing his friends,
finding those who would encourage him
to follow You. Strengthen him to live in
obedience to Your Word, and reward him
with a blameless reputation. Amen.

62

A Cheerful Outlook

May the righteous be glad and
rejoice before God; may they
be happy and joyful.
Psalm 68:3

Heavenly Father,

My son can easily forget Your goodness
and love. Set him free from the habits
of complaining and negative thinking.
Give him a cheerful outlook, happy in
knowing You're with him each day. Help
him to enjoy the love of his family and
friends, the talents he can develop, and
the gifts You lavish on his life. Fill him with
gratitude and praise for all You've done.
Amen.

63

Salvation through Jesus

Jesus answered, "I am the way and the
truth and the life. No one comes to the
Father except through Me."

John 14:6

Lord Jesus,

My son will wrestle with many choices for
coping with sin and pain in this world. Give
him faith to believe that Jesus is our only
hope for salvation. Let him commit his way
to following You. Enable him to understand
Your Word so he can know what's true.
Protect him when he's tempted to trust
in his own strength or false gods instead
of You alone. Use him to point the way to
God for those who are lost. Amen.

64

Spiritual Battles

Put on the full armor of God, so that
when the day of evil comes, you may be
able to stand your ground, and after you
have done everything, to stand.

Ephesians 6:13

Father,

Strengthen my son to stand his ground
against the enemy of his soul. Let him know
the Word and live in obedience to all You
command. Give him courage to declare
his faith in Jesus, trusting in You to save. Build
his faith in Your power and protection, and
keep him from fear when he suffers from evil
in this world. Make him faithful in prayer and
fill him with Your Spirit. Give him victory in his
struggle against the darkness. Amen.

65

Obeying the Word

Whoever looks intently into the perfect law that gives freedom, and continues in it – not forgetting what they have heard, but doing it – they will be blessed in what they do.

James 1:25

Lord,

The truth my son hears on Sunday can vanish from his memory by Monday. Let Your Word take root in his heart and mind. Teach him to live in the knowledge of You and Your will. Help him to obey Your commandments – to love You with all his heart, soul and mind, and to love his neighbor as himself. Bless him in everything he does as he studies the Scriptures and applies them to his life. Amen.

66

Loving Others

"Do to others as you would
have them do to you."
Luke 6:31

Lord Jesus,

My son can become so focused on
pleasing himself that he forgets to
care for others. Let him understand
the impact of his words and actions.
Help him to grow in thoughtfulness
and respect in our home and among
his friends. Enable him to be generous
and helpful, ready to share and take
turns. Teach him to play fair – able to
win or lose with a cheerful attitude.
Fill him with Your love. Amen.

67

Growth and Maturity

Let perseverance finish its work so
that you may be mature and complete,
not lacking anything.
James 1:4

Lord God,

Growing up is hard! Give my son endurance
to reach his goals, overcome sinful habits,
and deepen his knowledge of You. Motivate
him to leave childhood behind and pursue
maturity. Develop his initiative to pursue new
opportunities and friendships. Enable him
to understand Your Word so he can grow in
faith and obedience. Keep him from giving
up before he's the man You created him
to be. Amen.

68

Health and Well-Being

Dear friend, I pray that you may enjoy good
health and that all may go well with you,
even as your soul is getting along well.
3 John 2

Father,

The world is full of risk to my son's health,
safety and character. Protect him from
viruses and diseases that will steal his
strength. Keep him safe from accidents,
injuries, and attacks of every shape and
form. Fill him with Your Spirit, helping him to
know Your Word and to learn to pray. Grow
him up in physical vitality, wisdom and
security. Let him prosper in every way as
he lives in the shadow of Your wing. Amen.

69

Godly Mentors

Remember your leaders, who spoke the
word of God to you. Consider the outcome
of their way of life and imitate their faith.

Hebrews 13:7

Lord God,

My son needs godly men to set an
example for him to follow. Let him
see the healthy marriage of a loving
husband; the thriving children of a
dedicated father; the prosperous
career of a hard worker; the respected
leader of a church community; and
the peacemaker in a struggling
neighborhood. Reveal Your wisdom
and power through men who love You
and obey You wholeheartedly. Amen.

70

His Finances

Honor the Lord with your wealth, with the firstfruits of all your crops; then your barns will be filled to overflowing, and your vats will brim over with new wine.

Proverbs 3:9-10

Lord,

Thank You for providing for my son. Grow him in wisdom as he learns to handle his finances. Teach him to value each dollar as a gift from You. Reveal the mystery that generosity to others brings prosperity to his life. Let him give back to You as an act of worship and trust in Your provision. Be honored in his saving, spending and sharing. Show him Your limitless love through his blessings. Amen.

71

A Clean Conscience

I will praise the LORD, who counsels me;
even at night my heart instructs me. I keep
my eyes always on the LORD. With Him at my
right hand, I will not be shaken.

Psalm 16:7-8

Lord God,

My son needs to know right from wrong to
stay on the right path. Give him sensitivity to
hear and respond to the Spirit's direction.
Teach him the way of love and integrity.
Instruct his heart to know Your will and give
him strength to obey. Let him know the
security and peace that come from a
clean conscience. Keep him steady and
sure as he keeps his eyes on You. Amen.

72

A Man of His Word

Each of you must put off falsehood and
speak truthfully to your neighbor, for we
are all members of one body.
Ephesians 4:25

Heavenly Father,

Teach my son to be a man of his word.
Give him strength to keep his promises.
Keep him from bending the truth to protect
his reputation or to stay out of trouble. Turn
him away from every kind of deceit that
would break trust and destroy relationships.
Make him faithful – as You are faithful –
to speak the truth in love. Let his character
be defined by honesty and integrity
in all things. Amen.

73

His Character

Do not envy the violent or
choose any of their ways.
Proverbs 3:31

Lord,

Guys can be competitive, one-upping
each other in their quest to be number
one. Keep my son from aggression that
intimidates others and demands control.
Teach him restraint so he's gentle instead
of pushy and rough. Let him use words
instead of physical force to express his
emotions. Give him an aversion to violent
movies and entertainment that contradict
Your command to love. Fill him with
Your peace. Amen.

74

Eternal Life

"I give them eternal life, and they shall never perish; no one will snatch them out of My hand. My Father, who has given them to Me, is greater than all; no one can snatch them out of My Father's hand."

John 10:28-29

Father,

Thank You for the hope of eternal life together with You and the ones I love. Call my son to Yourself – give him salvation through believing in Jesus. Claim him as Your own so nothing can steal him from Your hand. Shield him from the enemy's schemes to cripple his faith and destroy his soul. Help him to trust in Your love that will never let him go. Amen.

75

Peaceful Sleep

In peace I will lie down and sleep, for You
alone, LORD, make me dwell in safety.

Psalm 4:8

Lord God,

When my son gets stressed out or
worried, he struggles to sleep. Give him
Your peace so he can find perfect rest.
Quiet his anxious thoughts and relax the
tension in his body. Reassure him in knowing that You never slumber or sleep –
You're watching over him every moment.
Let him rise refreshed and eager to
experience each new day. Amen.

76

Peer Pressure

Am I now trying to win the approval of
human beings, or of God? Or am I trying to
please people? If I were still trying to please
people, I would not be a servant of Christ.
Galatians 1:10

Father,

My son is wrestling over whom to
please – You, or the people around him.
Set him free from the pressure to fit in and
live up to others' expectations. Open his
eyes to see that outer appearances and
earthly trophies pass away in the end. Let
him pursue Your standard, seeking to love
and serve in Jesus' name. Reward his
obedience to You with peace and joy
in hearing, "Well done, good and
faithful servant." Amen.

77

Protection and Strength

Pray that we may be delivered from wicked
and evil people, for not everyone has faith.
But the Lord is faithful, and He will strengthen
you and protect you from the evil one.

2 Thessalonians 3:2-3

Holy Lord,

The enemy will attack my son and his faith
through the hatred of those that reject You.
Protect him from danger and persecution
for following You. Defend him from slander
and lies. Give him courage and hope, no
matter the opposition he suffers. Keep him
close through prayer and Your Word so that
he's always sure of Your truth. Comfort him
with Your love when he feels alone. Amen.

78

Loving God

Love the LORD your God with
all your heart and with all your
soul and with all your strength.
Deuteronomy 6:5

Holy Lord,

Our hearts turn away from You so easily.
Capture my son's emotions, giving him
joy when he discovers Your goodness.
Fill him with passion for the truth of Your
Word. Build up an unshakable faith in
Jesus – win his soul for You forever.
Give him courage and strength to obey
You, no matter what temptations and
opposition come his way. May he love
You without fail until he sees You face
to face. Amen.

79

Respect for Others

Do not rebuke an older man harshly, but exhort
him as if he were your father. Treat younger
men as brothers, older women as mothers, and
younger women as sisters, with absolute purity.

1 Timothy 5:1-2

Father,

Give my son a loving, proper relationship
with everyone in his life. Let him show
respect to the older generation – honoring
his grandparents and showing compassion
for the weakness of the elderly. Help him to
care for little ones without looking down on
their immaturity. Keep him from lust or
selfishness that insults young women.
Give him a humble heart that can learn
wisdom from all ages. Amen.

80

Diligence and Favor

May the favor of the Lord our God rest on us;
establish the work of our hands for us – yes,
establish the work of our hands.

Psalm 90:17

Lord,

It's discouraging for my son to work hard
without seeing results. Strengthen him to
keep on studying, valuing understanding
as much as the final grade. Help him to
persevere in building up skills to do work
he can be proud of. Let him show
integrity in every task he undertakes.
Bless his efforts to grow, learn and serve.
Establish a path toward prosperity
and independence. Amen.

81

The Consequences of Confession

If we claim to be without sin, we deceive ourselves and the truth is not in us. If we confess our sins, He is faithful and just and will forgive us our sins and purify us from all unrighteousness.

1 John 1:8-9

Holy Father,

When my son does something wrong, he is often so scared of what might happen that he makes up excuses and at times even denies what he's done. Humble his heart to admit his mistake. Help him to confess his wrongdoing and seek Your forgiveness. Set him free to enjoy a clean heart and a restored relationship with You. Give him joy and peace as he receives Your mercy. Thank You for Your gracious love. Amen.

82

Goals and Guidance

Commit to the LORD whatever you do,
and He will establish your plans. In their
hearts humans plan their course, but the
LORD establishes their steps.

Proverbs 16:3, 9

Father God,

My son is eager to make plans and take
on the world. He imagines the adventures
and success he'll have one day. Turn his
heart towards You, to seek Your perfect
will instead of his own way. Help him to
trust in Your goodness and wisdom for
his future. Keep him from running ahead
of Your timing – let him wait patiently for
direction. Teach him to hear Your voice
as You guide his steps. Amen.

83

Caring for the Earth

You are worthy, our Lord and God, to
receive glory and honor and power, for You
created all things, and by Your will they
were created and have their being.

Revelation 4.11

Lord,

You are the source of all life and the
beauty of the universe. Give my son
confidence to believe in You as his Creator.
Let him guard the well-being of the earth
and care for living things out of gratitude
for what You've made. Reveal Your eternal
power and divine nature to my son – let
him worship You as he's captivated by the
majesty of Your creation. Amen.

84

His Church Community

Let us consider how we may spur one another
on toward love and good deeds, not giving up
meeting together, as some are in the habit of
doing, but encouraging one another – and all
the more as you see the Day approaching.
Hebrews 10:24-25

Father,

You know we'll never be able to follow You
on our own. Thank You for the gift of Your
Church – a family to love, encourage, and
teach us along the way. Give my son a
deep commitment to Your people. Bind him
to a community of believers that will pour
Your love and wisdom into his life. Motivate
him to greater obedience through the godly
encouragement of other Christians. Amen.

85

Our Relationship

Be completely humble and gentle; be
patient, bearing with one another in love.
Make every effort to keep the unity of the
Spirit through the bond of peace.
Ephesians 4:2-3

Lord God,

Busy schedules, different personalities and
selfish desires can fracture my relationship
with my son. Keep us humble so we can
admit our mistakes. Help us to forgive when
we let each other down. Teach us to speak
and act out of love instead of our emotions.
Make us like-minded by Your Spirit – each
looking to care for the other and to obey
You in everything. Bind us together in love
and peace. Amen.

86

Comfort during Hardship

The LORD is close to the brokenhearted
and saves those who are crushed in spirit.

Psalm 34:18

Lord,

You know the pain my son has suffered.
Surround him with comfort and heal his
wounds. Rescue him from doubt and
discouragement that will devastate his
trust in You. Fill him with hope by Your Spirit
to believe that this trouble will pass and
that joy will come again. Help him to feel
Your presence as You're always by his side.
Amen.

87

Provision for His Needs

My God will meet all your needs according
to the riches of His glory in Christ Jesus.
Philippians 4:19

Holy Lord,

There's not always enough time, money or
strength to do what's before us each day.
Out of Your love, provide what's lacking for
my son. Crush every impossible obstacle
by Your might so he can move forward into
all You have in store. Everything on earth is
Yours – let my son see Your limitless power
to supply his needs. Increase his trust as he
finds You always faithful. Amen.

88

Avoiding Temptation

No temptation has overtaken you except what
is common to mankind. And God is faithful;
He will not let you be tempted beyond what you
can bear. But when you are tempted, He will also
provide a way out so that you can endure it.
1 Corinthians 10:13

Heavenly Father,

You know my son's struggle with
temptation – to satisfy his desires, put
himself first, and reject Your authority over
his life. Give him the strength to resist the
enticement of sin. Humble his heart to let
go of selfishness, and to care for others.
Help him to submit his words and actions
to You. In Your faithfulness, rescue him from
any disobedience that may damage his life
and turn him from following Jesus. Amen.

89

Purity and Innocence

I will not look with approval on anything that is vile. I hate what faithless people do; I will have no part in it. The perverse of heart shall be far from me; I will have nothing to do with what is evil.

Psalm 101:3-4

Father God,

My son's purity and innocence are constantly threatened in this broken world. Protect him from the destructive trap of pornography. Let him reject perversion, and love what's beautiful and holy. Give him strength to resist temptation and make wise choices. Show me how to set loving boundaries to protect my son's heart and mind. Keep him faithful and pure by the power of Your Spirit. Amen.

90

Bravery during Persecution

If you are insulted because of the name
of Christ, you are blessed, for the Spirit
of glory and of God rests on you.
1 Peter 4:14

Lord God,

Give my son courage to follow You, no
matter what it may cost. Let him be willing
to give up popularity and acceptance to
live for You. Repay every insult and hardship
with blessings from heaven. Reveal Your
glory in his life as he honors You at all times.
Keep him close and strengthen him to
endure in a world that denies Your name.
Thank You for Your love and the hope of
what's to come. Amen.

91

New Challenges

For the Spirit God gave us does not
make us timid, but gives us power,
love and self-discipline.

2 Timothy 1:7

Father,

My son needs courage to face what's
ahead. Give him Your power to tackle
new challenges without shrinking back.
Strengthen him to love the lonely, the
weak and the unpopular. Overcome his
insecurities so he can boldly reach out
and make friends. Keep distraction and
fatigue from hindering his diligence and
hard work. Make him strong by Your Spirit
to do whatever You ask. Amen.

92

Our Family's Faith

These commandments that I give you today
are to be on your hearts. Impress them on
your children. Talk about them when you sit
at home and when you walk along the road,
when you lie down and when you get up.

Deuteronomy 6:6-7

Lord Jesus,

Fill our home with the truth of Your Word.
Give me strength to faithfully teach my son
to follow You. Saturate our conversations
with godly wisdom. Show us how to apply
the Scriptures to our struggles and questions.
Lead us to pray together for our needs, and
to praise You for Your goodness to our
family. Create a lasting legacy of faith
in our household. Amen.

93

Good Judgment

The simple believe anything, but the
prudent give thought to their steps.
Proverbs 14:15

Heavenly Father,

Give my son wisdom to know what is true
or false, sensible or foolish. Protect him
from following others into danger. Guard
him from embarrassing choices that
would harm his reputation. Shield him from
schemes that promise a blessing but lead
to hardship and pain. Sharpen his vision
to recognize darkness disguised as light.
Lead him in Your truth every day. Amen.

94

His Struggles

We know that in all things God works for
the good of those who love Him, who have
been called according to His purpose.

Romans 8:28

Holy Lord,

Comfort my son with Your promise to turn
today's struggles into tomorrow's reward.
Use frustration to teach him endurance.
Let disappointment evolve into gratitude
for even better gifts that You have in mind.
Give him confidence in the future,
believing You will do more than he can
ask or imagine. Use every heartache and
hardship to draw him into the love of Jesus,
who gave Himself up for us. Amen.

95

Success and Prosperity

Wealth and honor come from You; You are the
ruler of all things. In Your hands are strength
and power to exalt and give strength to all.
1 Chronicles 29:12

Lord,

You are the source of our well-being and
success. Strengthen my son to work hard
and prosper. Provide discernment for his
choices and relationships. Equip him to be
a godly leader – courageous, humble and
wise – to build up others and point them
to You. Entrust my son with resources and
responsibility as he obeys You in everything.
Let him honor You as You lift him up. Amen.

96

When He Is Lost

"Suppose one of you has a hundred sheep
and loses one of them. Doesn't he leave
the ninety-nine in the open country and go
after the lost sheep until he finds it?"
Luke 15:4

Father,

Thank You for sending Jesus to seek and save
the lost. Pursue my son when he drifts away
from You and bring him home. When he
gets blinded by confusion and sin, open his
eyes to see how much he needs Your
salvation. Give me faith to believe that
You're in control. Help me to patiently trust
in Your love that never fails. Thank You
for Your power to save. Amen.

97

A Spiritual Heritage

I will sing of the LORD's great love forever;
with my mouth I will make Your faithfulness
known through all generations.

Psalm 89:1

Lord God,

Even now, prepare my son to be a man of
God. Help me to teach him Your Word and
to encourage his walk with You as he grows.
Enable him to lead his family in worship and
wisdom. Let his belief in Jesus take hold in
his children's hearts as well. Let the story of
salvation in his life be told for generations.
Claim our family as Your own – create a
heritage of faith that never ends. Amen.

98

A Pure Marriage in Future

Marriage should be honored by all, and the
marriage bed kept pure, for God will judge
the adulterer and all the sexually immoral.

Hebrews 13:4

Father,

You created marriage to be a refuge of
lifelong love and faithfulness. When my
son does get married, protect him from
the schemes of the enemy, luring him to
sexual sin. Keep him free from adultery,
pornography and lust. Let intimacy with
his wife be beautiful and pure, and let
nothing separate them or ruin their love.
Amen.

99

Devotion to God

Jesus answered, "It is written: 'Worship the Lord your God and serve Him only.'"

Luke 4:8

Lord,

Countless idols compete for my son's heart. May he worship and serve You alone. Give him a desire to please You when he's tempted to fit in with the crowd. Satisfy him with all You've given him when he craves material things. Help him to hold on to Your truth when confronted with the world's religions and philosophies. Let his allegiance to Christ never waver or fade. Amen.

100

Physical Healing

Heal me, LORD, and I will be healed;
save me and I will be saved, for
You are the one I praise.
Jeremiah 17:14

Lord,

When my son gets sick and discouraged,
relieve his pain and restore his strength by
Your healing power. Bind his wounds, cure
his diseases, and bring peace to his heart
as his perfect Physician. Fill him with praise
as he experiences Your saving love and
healing touch. Amen.

101

Love and Peace

The LORD is compassionate and gracious,
slow to anger, abounding in love.
Psalm 103:8

Father God,

Give me Your heart of love for my son.
Fill me with compassion for his weaknesses,
and patience with his immaturity. Keep me
from anger and resentment when he fails.
Help me to forgive the past and hold on to
hope for his future. Use my gracious words,
serving hands and wise leadership to reveal
Your goodness to my son. May the merciful
love of Jesus bind us together and give us
peace. Amen.